Reflections on Aging
Greeting the Changing Face in the Mirror

Essays
Bruce McBeath, Ph.D.

Photography
Robin Wipperling

P. Hanson Marketing
Layout and Design: Joan D. Loesch
1407 West Fourth Street | Red Wing, Minnesota 55066
651-385-3372

Contents

Introduction

The inner experience of growing older

The most exciting news about growing older comes to us straight from the interior life of older people. This is not to discount how much the "outside view" drawn from statistics about aging helps us discover how we can live longer and healthier lives by, for example, paying more attention to important lifestyle changes like exercise and nutrition.

This is all to the good, but even the helpful knowledge we draw from statistics misses the core changes associated with healthy aging. These important shifts in our experience arise within us, an internal "hidden dimension" that marks substantial changes in how we perceive, think and feel, what we most value, and in our significant life concerns. In this regard, even physical illness or disability does not preclude our experience of a "healthy" older age.

It is the view from the inside of aging, the "lived experience of growing older" that compels this collection of essays and photographs. Knowing about the interior life of older people has substantially challenged many of our assumptions about aging, and helps re-shape our perspective about this culminating period of our life. Healthy older people, we find, experience life in ways beyond the capacity of those caught in ordinary "adulthood" to imagine or perceive. We are encouraged to think and feel differently about growing older as we become more aware of how older age is experienced by those actually living it! Hidden inside the obvious physical changes most visible to younger people lies the complexity and unceasing simplicity that marks a primary paradox of aging.

We want to identify these life changes, and intend these photographic images to illumine and expand the themes captured within these essays. We present no "pie in the sky" fabrications about growing older, but rather vignettes drawn from the "lived experience" of people we have been fortunate to know as seasoned veterans of aging. Some of the descriptions you find here may surprise, and perhaps please you as aging is shown to be a harvest of maturity, wisdom, and emotional ripening. This glimpse into healthy aging demonstrates that the last phase of life is every bit as interesting and exciting an adventure as any that came before it. We invite you to take a look, and see for yourself.

Chapter One

The truth beyond the lies: Healthy aging

Healthy aging requires that we actively engage our minds, our emotions, our physical bodies, and our spirits. We have not been taught to do this. In fact, we have been taught a dreadful series of hurtful ideas about aging.

Healthy aging requires that we must first (and foremost) actively reject the lies we've been told about being old!

opinions are often elegant and profound

Let's discard some stereotypes

Taking an honest look at the process of aging means, right at the start, that we discard some important falsehoods. Here are some antiquated stereotypes we immediately nominate for the discard pile.

"Older brains don't work as well as younger ones do."

Not true. Healthy older brains work differently. For example, processing information more selectively, with deeper and more integrative thinking. With age, some elements of cognitive speed are sacrificed for depth. If you want fast and shallow thinking – stay young!

"Older people are more emotionally upset than younger people."

Not true by a long shot. Healthy older people actually report greater experiences of contentment with their lives than do their juniors. Looking for emotional turmoil? Try adolescence!

"Wisdom always comes with age."

Often true, but clearly not always the case. Healthy aging involves deeper understanding and greater compassion for others. Unfortunately, some people stuck in rigid and inflexible mindsets in their younger years may continue to live in the same mental ruts as they grow older. Aging, in and of itself, is no guarantee of wisdom.

"You can't teach an old dog new tricks."

Way wrong. Older adults actually require new learning to keep their brains healthy. Learning "new tricks" takes practice and patience for people of any age. But healthy older people are learning new stuff all the time, from new languages and the use of new technologies to complex skills involving the body and the brain, like woodworking, quilting, and dancing. Because older adults have more life experience to bring to the task of learning something new, teachers often regard these students as among their most interesting and satisfying.

"Older people are set in their ways."

The idea that older people are inflexible and unable to accept new information or adapt to new circumstances is a variation of the above, and is proven false by the countless number of healthy older people who have brought radical new ideas into the world. Because older people take more time to process information, and process it more deeply (in part, the experience factor), their resulting ideas and opinions are often elegant and profound.

These seriously flawed stereotypes are highlighted whenever we match them against the actual life experience of healthy older adults. What others would you add to the discard pile?

"facts" for the dust bin of history

As we learn about aging, what other "facts" will fall?

Even more of the "facts" used to describe the experience of aging have recently been tested and invalidated. The presumed "facts" describing inevitable cognitive decline in older years or the automatic loss of memory with age have now been subjected to scientific scrutiny and found to be false.

Some research on aging actually confirms the exact opposite of what we had supposed to be "true." Emotional stability is a case in point. The "facts" describing emotional turmoil as a consequence of aging has 'in fact' been turned on its head, as research repeatedly demonstrates that older people lead all other age groups in emotional maturity and stability.

On the basis of this upheaval in our understanding of aging, there are good grounds for us to shake our head and wonder "what's the next 'fact' to fall?" Some are already well on their way to the dust bin of history. Here are just two important examples:

> Older workers are not as effective and productive as younger ones.

> The emerging truth: evaluative reviews assessing the "value added" potential of older workers have challenged this outmoded perspective. We now know that older workers characteristically bring emotional stability, dependability and reliability with them into the workplace.

> Older people are "stuck" in their ways and resistant to change.

> The emerging truth: older people are more complex thinkers, and integrate values based on life experience into their perspectives. They know that "newer" does not always equal "better" and "older" does not necessarily equal "worse." They know, too, that "happiness," beyond certain narrow limits, is not a consequence of having more material possessions. Sometimes "resisting change" is just such an expression of an integrated, time-tested, and value-based perspective that clashes with some contemporary cultural influences.

That brings us to another important emerging truth about aging: people become increasingly unique as they age.

This makes older adults the most complex and diverse collection of individuals within the human population, more difficult to categorize or label than any other age group. Knowing this helps us understand why some "facts" fit some older people and not others, and why no labels or generalizations work very well when attempting to describe the experience of older adults.

Believing, we make it so

Through the course of our lives we have been encouraged to form many false beliefs about aging, but how dangerous can this be? Truth be told, it turns out that our personal beliefs about aging have a dramatic impact on what happens to us as we grow older, with consequences that can be quite harmful and disruptive.

While we have long known that our personal belief system affected our mental and physical health, what we have more recently learned is how our personal beliefs impact our process of aging and our longevity. And their impact is huge!

Recent research tells the tale: Yale researchers asked people over 50 if they agreed with the popular stereotypes about aging: that you don't have energy anymore, that your body breaks down rapidly, that you're no longer useful, and that older people are unhappy. Then the researchers followed these people for over two decades to see how they aged and how long they lived.

Here's what they found: people who refused to believe the popular negative stereotypes about aging in fact lived healthier lives, and lived on average seven-and-one half years longer than people who believed the negative stereotypes were true! They discovered that what we believe about getting older has more impact on how we age and on our length of life than just about anything else we can do to live a healthy life; more than diet does, or exercise, or our cholesterol levels, or our weight, or whether or not we smoke. Of course all of these are important, but our beliefs about aging have the most powerful impact over all the other factors.

This study shows us how our process of aging tends to mirror what we believe about getting older. We need to beware the negative stereotypes that are, indeed, dangerous to our health.

Let's replace them with these tested positive descriptions of aging that lead to greater health and longer life:

✦ as we age we deepen our interests and exercise our creativity

✦ we are active and engaged with our friends

✦ we contribute to our community

✦ we use the freedom and maturity that age brings to live more meaningful lives.

Let's celebrate the beliefs that affirm our real experience and nourish our lives as older adults.

the impact of our beliefs is huge

be careful about what we believe

Testing the power of our beliefs

We have been reviewing how we are surrounded by stereotypes that impact how we age. Many of these stereotypes are negative and damaging. For example, to be older means to be less proficient than before, to have impaired cognition, and to have problems with memory. Consequently, when we view ourselves as "older," we run the real risk of also taking on the negative stereotypes that accompany that label. Doing this has disastrous consequences, indeed!

Recent research in the field of aging continues to confirm the fact that what we believe about aging has enormous power regarding how well or poorly we function as we age. A new study looked closely at how a broad range of older adults performed on tasks related to memory and to general cognitive functioning like thinking and problem solving. They assessed how well people performed after exposing them to these common negative stereotypes. Some people were encouraged to consider themselves "older" and then given selected "information" suggesting that older people often had more memory problems, or had more difficulty with thinking or problem solving. These people actually demonstrated significantly more difficulty with the memory and cognitive tasks they were given to perform. Other people who were the same age or even older and were not given the combination of the label "older" with the negative expectations about aging, showed no such deterioration on these same measures of memory or cognitive functioning.

These studies show us just how powerfully disabling negative stereotypes of aging are on the lives of older adults. We see how someone who believes older people will have problems with their thinking can actually perform poorly if tested for dementia. A poor evaluation can reinforce a negative stereotype and a personal disaster. Healthcare professionals testing for memory loss or dementia in older populations may harbor these same negative stereotypes themselves, only confirming the negative result they are already expecting to find.

What we believe to be true about aging guides and supports our personal expectations about how we will function as we grow older. We see with shocking clarity the power our beliefs have when we look at research studies like this. These are cautionary tales that tell us to be careful about what we believe, lest we, by believing it, make it so.

Healthcare biases
diminish us

To claim that our health care system does not meet the needs of older adults surprises no one. Many older people have had the experience of going to see a doctor who diagnoses their ailment as "old age." Many more have had the experience of feeling rushed in a medical appointment, uncertain about what to report or how to describe their concerns to their doctor in the few minutes available to them in the exam room. A stumbling confusion about how to comply with the recommendations they receive is also a familiar experience for many.

But "you're getting older" is not a diagnosis—it is a prejudicial statement at once both lame and ageist. Some physicians have long recognized this, and have fought hard to provide adequate care to their older patients. They know that older patients often have more complex medical histories, and require more time to communicate and understand what is going on with their bodies. Due to metabolic changes, older patients are often more sensitive to medication reactions, and commonly need careful monitoring of possible drug interactions if they are receiving multiple medications. This takes time, and the careful and caring attention of their doctor.

How, then, do we older adults find the care we need within a medical system that too often seems rigged against us? One feisty geriatrician (an M.D. trained both as an internist and in geriatric medicine) talks about this and tells us how. In his book, *Treat Me, Not My Age,* Mark Lachs, M.D. takes on the valuable job of describing how to navigate our modern health care system, and find (or hang onto) a doctor who will see the individual "you" behind your years.

Dr. Lachs is a strong advocate for older people getting the care they need, and for those working within our health care system to eliminate the kind of ageism that prevents good care. But he also recognizes that we older patients also have the responsibility to better advocate for ourselves. We need to search out good information, and be willing to speak more frankly and openly with the health care professionals who are there to serve us. We are critical members of the medical team that helps improve the quality of care for all older people.

"you're getting older" is not a diagnosis

Embracing the "older person" label

Even common words that identify and define us can convey serious distortions and easily become barriers. In the present day, being labeled an "old person" can imply a kind of inferior status as a person. Indeed, our very fear of being viewed as "old" can lock us out of involvement with many resources most helpful to us.

According to the commonly held contemporary view, to be old is associated with being decrepit, non-productive, "out of it," a fogey, a codger, weak and helpless. More positive terms like "senior citizen" fail to erase the meaning this label has acquired in today's ageist and youth oriented culture. Only rarely do you hear older people promoted as the great social resource that we actually are. When only young people in our culture are promoted as "society's hope," it's no wonder those of us toward the other end of the age continuum want to dodge the "older person" label as long as we can.

Yet there are consequence to our reluctance to fully embrace our "older person" status. One big one is that we unwittingly help perpetuate the misguided and harmful labeling of older people. How many otherwise interested and engaged older people speak of avoiding participating in some community activities or social programs because these were for "really old people," certainly not for them! Doesn't our non-participation encourage the negative, even cataclysmic, stereotype of aging as if aging were the equivalent of dying?

We can choose to dodge this "older" label, or we can wear it openly and correct the image others have of the kind of life and experience that it signifies. Because we older adults are less distracted with the tasks associated with raising families and building careers, we can more readily follow our own interests and curiosity. We can choose to offer our service to our community and participate in the process of tapping society's most valuable untapped resource (us).

We erode the negative label about aging whenever we bring our energy and vitality into the lives of others in our community. We change perceptions of aging by providing direct evidence about how older people actually think, believe, and behave and we teach our younger, more "junior citizens" that growth and maturity continue throughout life.

we can wear it openly

Proven models for changing times

The philosopher Nietzsche observed that whatever doesn't destroy us makes us stronger. Although he didn't say so, he must have had older people in mind! With the experience of living through life's changing phases and facing hardship and adversity as it comes along, older people have an emotional strength and resilience that makes even the so-called "ravages of age" more tolerable.

Does this characterization have a "Pollyanna-like" ring to it? Actually this picture is backed up by some good scientific evidence. Recent and frequently repeated research shows how older people demonstrate more balance and stability in their mood, are generally more optimistic and cheerful, and recover more quickly from experiences of disappointment or loss than younger people do. While emotional upheaval is standard fare for adolescents and young adults, the oldest generation most often reports the highest measure of contentment among any age group.

Curiously, the process of aging is associated in the minds of many people with resisting change and being "stuck in the past." However, the capacity to face change and adversity, and successfully adjust to major transitions in living is exactly what older people do routinely. Older people have lived through social, political, and technological changes that younger people can scarcely imagine, from world wars and early automobiles to computers and the formation of a new and tension filled geopolitical global community. Moreover, when we look at how older adults characteristically cope with the increasing occasions of loss and infirmity in their personal lives, we are heartened by the quality of character that shines through their resilience. We see how much strength and courage older people muster in the face of difficulties that can simply overwhelm people much younger.

The strength, courage, and endurance expressed by older adults as they cope with change reflects the accrual of character, built over a lifetime of meeting life's challenges and demands. Our contemporary society is even now in the throes of transition and cries out for role models to help guide important continuing social and cultural changes today. Where are the living models of emotional strength, courage, and persistence in the face of the challenges that confront us today?

They are right here, in the lives and character displayed by so many elders living in our midst. Just look around!

our character shines through

Honor the changing face in the mirror

How sad it is that we are not taught to seek out the beauty in the faces of older people. Our youth obsessed culture encourages us to worship the smooth baby face of the young and pack older, wrinkled skin off to the cosmetic surgeon to banish all traces of age.

Our cultural emphasis on youthful beauty was not always nearly so dominant. In many places and times it was the faces of the elders that have enshrined the ideal of beauty and stood as a proud testament to the fullness of life. In our contemporary world, however, we have far too little encouragement to celebrate the physical beauty associated with aging.

The influence of these broader cultural forces existing around us can interrupt and certainly complicate our continuing acceptance of our own aging body. When we look at the aging face that is reflected back to us in the mirror each morning, we may be too prone to see ourselves through the lens of our surrounding youth oriented culture. Then, acceptance of this map of our personal history that is written across our cheeks, forehead, chin and neck becomes something to be changed rather than to be treasured.

Yet a cultural attitude that attaches physical beauty only to youth flies in the face of what we are learning about the real experience of aging. One primary and positive attribute of aging is an increased capacity to accept and treasure life "as it is," in its various manifestations. This attribute is usually underdeveloped and hard to find in the more often self critical reactions of younger and middle aged people. Older people, with typically more developed sensitivity, can see beauty in the faces of young and old. With the advantage of age, we are able to see in our own aging face a fascinating mapping of experiences in living through many chapters of life. Beauty is found in the lines and wrinkles that mark our movement through love and loss, success and disappointment, growth and change through time.

These tracings of personal history we find reflected in our mirrors each morning affirm the life and experience of each older person residing inside that image. They signify a life not to be disregarded or erased, but to be acknowledged, accepted and celebrated.

seek out the beauty

23

Chapter Two

Metamorphosis—
Aging and changing

As older adults, we are not the persons we were years ago—we are now so much more! The exterior changes in our bodies are more than matched by those that occur inside us, in a complex expansion of our minds and the immense refinement of our emotions.

We now face the great task of bringing the harvest of our aging out of the fields and into our everyday lives. How well does our outer life now reflect our changing, maturing self?

Housecleaning for a new chapter of life

If there were a neon sign wired into psyches of older adults to record their most prominent fears, "useless" and "good for nothing" would likely be flashing a lot.

These particular fears can bubble up suddenly and tromp the living daylights out of whatever thread of life satisfaction had been around before. Gone is the good feeling of being "grandpa" or "grandma" to someone, or to sweet remembrances of times past. In their place now only a pit of despair: "I used to be useful...I used to be important...I used to matter...I used to be able to..."

What a tight circle we weave when we rocket from "used to's" to "useless," from nostalgia to despair. And what a tragedy to have so much of our creative energy and the seeds of new possibility, the now heralded gifts associated with aging, cut off in this way.

When we take a closer look at this pattern, we often find that the inner freedom we sought to achieve through independence from work and rearing children is now crowded out by the still lingering attachments we had formed to the various roles, positions, and responsibilities that gave our lives meaning when we were younger. But now these vestiges of earlier life have outlived their usefulness, and need to be released.

When we release them we may find ourselves left with a sense of uncertainty and ambiguity. Rightly so, since this is how "freedom" initially feels. When we let go of vestiges of our past, we don't simply receive a developed picture of how we are now. It is far more likely that releasing old expectations simply nets us uncluttered space into which something new can emerge within us. We need to abide the tension uncertainty brings long enough to nurture that newer "something" along.

This is a vital process that calls for an interior kind of housecleaning—clearing out the old images of our earlier life and releasing the expectations associated with them. When we exercise our freedom to choose (really choose) what has meaning for us at this older age, we are doing the purposeful work of aging. May we now give energy and attention to what we find or create in this new chapter of our lives!

clear out old images—create new space

emotional maturity is revealed in older years

Improving with age,
we live inspiring lives

Older adults are the clear leaders in emotional health. Today we have plenty of solid research that shows how older adults advance beyond any other age group in indicators of emotional maturity. Openness to new experiences, acceptance of others and generosity are traits found most often in healthy older adults.

One striking example demonstrating how emotional maturity is revealed in older years can be found in the life of Huston Smith. He's a philosopher and historian of world religions whose work has attracted a considerable audience of scholars and thinkers who have followed him over a number of years. Recently, at age 90, Smith elected to enter an assisted living facility, not wanting to burden his family with his care. Of that decision, he said: "People go to nursing homes, I've heard it said, to die. I came to this assisted-living residence, it seems, to cheer people up."

Smith writes in his autobiography, *Tales of Wonder: Adventures Chasing the Divine*, about how he seeks to improve the daily experience of those around him. "I could obsess about my ailments and be an old man in misery," he writes. "Instead I forget them and wonder how I came to be so fortunate" (to be living in this facility, and with these people).

The most important point about Huston Smith's experience is that when we examine it closely, it is not exceptional. When we carefully review the experience of healthy older adults living into their ninth and tenth decades of life, we can find many similar examples of this strong level of social interest in others, with this same spirit of generosity, and cheerful helpfulness. This gentle loving attitude can even shine through the physical pain and limitations that may also be present for these courageous and caring elders.

Perhaps because of his life long attraction to religion, Huston Smith describes his experience in terms of faith. "As I enter my tenth decade on earth, my faith...coming out of my experience... seem to be enlarging." Doesn't he capture something that is available to us all as we mature in age?

Our worth as a person changes

Struggling with questions about our value, or worth as a person, is a common experience for any older person. Because we are no longer actively "producing and providing" through work, or raising a family, we can tell ourselves that we now have little if any continuing significance. We may have spent a lifetime defining our personal value by the success we were able to achieve, or what we were able to "do." When we are done with "doing" as a measure of our worth as a person, where does that leave us? Perhaps worthless and without value?

As older adults, we face the challenge of separating "worth" from "work." Yet the process of confusing these is an old habit, one reinforced by the messages we receive from our culture that we are only as good as our last paycheck. Our value as a person (our "beingness") has long been fused together with our capacity to be productive (our "doingness"). These are the standards by which younger people are encouraged to measure themselves centered on their ability to perform, to accomplish, and to "do things." They are, however, woefully inaccurate measures when applied to the life of any older person.

If we are to now assess ourselves based on a standard of "being," we must recognize that our core value comes from our humanness, from who we are, not from what we can accomplish. Some of the dimensions of our "being" include our capacity to love and be with others, to experience and express creativity and beauty, and to appreciate and care for this world in a variety of ways. It is our "beingness" that we express when we move through each day showing respect for life, and demonstrating that by treating others with kindness and compassion.

It is often said, even from a non-religious viewpoint, "this is God's world and we are God's children." This statement conveys the value of our "beingness" and encourages us to acknowledge the singular importance of our one unique existence with its interesting changes and ongoing development. As older adults, we point others the way toward a life that goes beyond external "achievement" into the very heart of being more fully human.

when we're done with "doing," who are we?

Choosing our attitude

You might wonder about this. Can our attitude actually be chosen? Isn't it just something that arises out of the life circumstances in which we find ourselves?

Actually, no. The evidence for the fact that we choose our attitude can be seen by simply looking at the lives of different people around us. We might find people with very difficult life circumstances who appear remarkably cheerful and engaging. We also might find people who have much more comfortable life circumstances and yet are filled with grumbles and complaints. We might notice people with significant health problems who remain pleasant, attentive and caring, and others with relatively good health whose aches and pains color much of their experience of life.

Clearly anyone who has progressed to any older and more mature age has lived through a vast mixture of positive and negative life experiences, through some better times and worse times. We have all had important relationships with some fine people, and with some real skunks. On top of that, we have all probably had experiences that were quite painful and that we'd rather forget and certainly not repeat. All of us also have days when we're "off our game" and project a more sour and grumpy mood than usual. But these infrequent changes in our mood are usually temporary, unlike an underlying attitude toward life that remains more stable.

Now, as "seasoned" adults, we continue an ongoing process of attitude forming whenever we select pieces of our daily experience and place our attention on them. Whether we know it or not, the attitude we form is a consequence of the choices we make. When we place our attention on parts of our experience that we find nurturing, comforting, or pleasing, we contribute to an attitude that reflects comfort and care to others. When we place our attention mainly on the pain or distress that has been present in our life, we will tend to contribute to a sour attitude that can feel poisonous to those around us.

Each day each of our lives contain some mixture of pleasant and unpleasant experiences. Will we select gratitude, kindness and compassion as our focus in building the attitude we display to others, or will we select anger, jealousy or resentment. That choice is always ours.

the choice is always ours

"tough stuff" is part of the whole

"Aging whole" is not without pain

A good friend and colleague is now well into her mid-80's and continues to be professionally active because, she says, "I just love what I do." This elegant and spirited woman has epitomized, for many, what it means to "have it all together." Apart from some hip pain, from an outsiders' perspective she has lead a blessed existence throughout her adulthood. Even a more intimate observer of her life over the past several decades would most likely carry that impression as well.

But when we lean in a little closer to glimpse her life below the surface, the picture gets more complicated. She takes on a more somber and reflective tone as she responds to an inquiry about her family. She describes how her daughter, a talented, highly trained and skilled professional woman, struggles with a seriously debilitating, chronic disease. "You know," she tells us, "I'm in my eighties and I have more physical ability now than my daughter does, and she's barely fifty. It doesn't seem right that parents live well when their children have to suffer."

As we continue to talk about our lives, our work, and our children, she brightens again. She becomes more animated as she tells about an upcoming trip to Europe, and we notice how, although her very real sadness about her daughter's illness is not far from the surface, she has not lost contact with other experiences, other "realities" that she carries inside that are sources of satisfaction and pleasure.

How does someone "aging well" experience the whole of their life? Given what we know and understand about this woman, we would imagine her to be a model of "successful aging." Yet she has not arrived at this older point in her life unscathed. Clearly, she has real and continuing pain, both in relation to her daughter and in her body. But she is aging well because she is "aging whole." She is integrating the really "tough stuff" in her life into the larger totality of her life without diminishing any individual piece. Real sadness and real pain are blended with real pleasure and real joy. She owns all of her experience in living and appears to cast none of it aside. In this, she presents us with an inspiring portrait of aging.

Let's look at our memory

You forget where you put your reading glasses for about the third time that day. And now, what did you do with the car keys when you came in? You know that book you were reading is around here somewhere, but where? And where's that other glove? Who did you say you'd call back later today? Are you losing your mind, or what? Frustrating!

No, the strong likelihood is that you're not losing your mind. Rather, you're experiencing something that happens to all of us to some degree or another, as we grow older. We tend to forget or misplace things more often. We also find it harder to juggle a number of things in our minds at the same time without dropping at least one of them.

Some memory researchers believe that, with aging, the real issue isn't so much that we remember less but rather that we can't multi-task, or divide our attention between several different concerns as well as we formerly thought that we could. From this perspective, forgetting is more about careful focus and attention and less about our having some kind of erosion of our memory.

Another factor is our more expanded history in living. Simply put, we have many more "memory files" than a younger person does. We actually may remember quite well, but require more time to find the right spot in our larger storage vault!

Stress is also an important factor. Stress affects our capacity to process information and to retain it. When we're fatigued or stressed our capacity to remember is compromised. As we're more relaxed, our capacity to remember is more likely to be most effective. This is why it's so important to not berate ourselves when we forget something. If we do, we add pressure and increase the likelihood that we will have an even harder time remembering. In fact, recent studies have shown that older people who did poorly on timed tests actually did as well or better than college students when the pressure of time is removed.

Let's remove the pressure of time by allowing ourselves to forget, to relax, and to practice compassion for these rather ordinary lapses in memory as they might occur. Being comfortable with forgetting helps us remain relaxed, and improves our capacity to remember.

stress affects our capacity to remember

Aging with less risk and more reward

For younger people, risky behavior usually involves acts of commission: drug and alcohol abuse, reckless driving, sexual involvements, and the like. But for us older adults, at risk behaviors more often result from acts of omission than from acts of commission – it is not so much the dangerous things we do that hurt us; it is, rather, the important things we fail to do to that put us at risk. Actions and activities that are necessary to support and sustain physical and mental wellness are avoided, forgotten or ignored.

Through passivity and inattention, many older adults put themselves at risk without even recognizing they are doing so. We place our physical health at risk by ignoring the necessary regular physical exercise required to support strength and flexibility. We know it's "use it or lose it" at older ages, but passivity and procrastination trump the self-commitment required to start an exercise program. Physical health is often further impaired through inadequate nutrition, as self neglect trumps self care. Older adults living alone are especially prone to having poor diets and irregular meals, a further invitation to medical issues.

Then there is the risk of diminished social networks through the death of friends and loved ones, something that impacts all of us older adults. Our network of friends and close relations is our primary "social insurance" against loneliness and social isolation. Consequently, making new friends and actively nourishing our social network is an ongoing necessity. When we turn away from possible new friendships and become inattentive to our relationships we place ourselves at greater risk of a future filled with despondency and loneliness.

Finally, there is the care of our mind: to maintain a healthy brain and a vital mind requires that we exercise our capacity to learn throughout the course of our lives. We keep our minds supple and alive by expanding our knowledge and encouraging our interests. Whenever we shun new learning, we place ourselves at risk of living in a dramatically diminished world.

These acts of omission that place us at risk can each day be converted to positive acts of nurture and self care. We can make a new series of choices: for exercise, diet, social connection, and mental stimulation. In this day, what will you choose?

acts of omission place us at risk

every decision is borne alone

The challenge of the single life for older adults

Our basic need for safety and security creates in us a compelling desire for stable relationships. We settle into patterns of activity and intimacy with a spouse, family and close friends that may hardly vary for decades. These relationships become a protective skin that makes the pain and unpredictability of life more tolerable. The loss of a spouse or partner through death or divorce destroys that skin and turns everything on its head, leaving the surviving partner feeling like an alien in a foreign land – not just alone, but lost and vulnerable as well.

Suddenly, where life was comfortably fitted into a coupled world, there is singleness – a "onesey" without a "twosey" as someone in exactly that situation termed it. Every experience in life now feels different—every decision is borne alone, from each rearrangement of furniture to how to structure the day. Negotiating social relationships, once part of a routine, now becomes complicated and difficult, indeed often the hardest aspect of this new (and so often unwanted), single life.

Those of us standing on the outside and watching someone struggle with this kind of loss can well understand the pressure and desire some feel to recouple quickly, to bury their loss and painful loneliness in another relationship as soon as possible. For many older adults, the loss of a spouse presents the surviving partner with their first real experience of being "on their own." Many older people have had minimal experience with any kind of single life until the death of their spouse, and consequently take on two new and unwelcome experiences simultaneously: profound loss and being a first time single.

A single person's already heightened sense of vulnerability is further compounded by the nature of the remarkable different world any older single person encounters today. There is great risk of sliding into social isolation in this more anonymous society where so much of our communication with others has been replaced by machines. Missing the personal affirmation provided by simple daily encounters with others, older singles work hard to avoid withdrawing and isolating to protect against what can feel like a chilly and forbidding social climate. Having lost the protective skin of couplehood, encountering life as an older single requires real courage.

Reaching out to others

Our mental health takes a nosedive when we become socially isolated. When we're isolated from others, we're more likely to feed on negative thoughts that reinforce despair and leave us with a sense of hopelessness. We are also more likely to be less attentive to good nutrition, exercise, and sleep habits that contribute to our general health.

What makes social isolation especially troublesome is that it's so easy to stay separated from other people at the very times when we most need good, supportive social contact to feel better. When we feel sad, "blue," with some tinge of self-doubt or despair, we can very easily remain passive and withdrawn. We want to just shut the door and turn off the world, with little emotional energy motivating us to be active and engaging with others.

Breaking out of this pattern of isolation takes energy that we often don't feel we have. Our energy for people contact can be sucked up by the heavy "down" feelings that work against reaching out, and it takes some courageous effort on our part to not succumb to these feelings. We defy our own inner resistance when we simply approach a friend or neighbor that we consider a "safe person" and start a conversation with them. And we magnificently "disobey" our negative feelings and help ourselves enormously when we allow ourselves to tell that "safe person" something about how we're feeling inside. Just a tiny bit of disclosing our feelings opens us to connection, and takes us one big step out of isolation.

We know we need to reach out when we're cut off from others, and also know that we can't count on our feelings to help us when we're captured in a negative, heavy mood. But we can count on what we know will work to help us begin to feel better. We can identify a person or persons who we believe will be "safe people" for us. We can decide to reach out to them, even in small ways, and begin a conversation. We understand that we take these steps, not because we "feel like it" (we don't), but because this is one practical path to feeling better and less isolated. Even knowing that we are not "feeling up to it," we do it anyway.

when we want to turn off the world

Dancing with summer in autumn's body

It's nice weather, and we want to be outside, doing something active like we long have done. But our now older bodies are sometimes stressed by physical problems that make it harder to work and play in just the way we had before.

We are aware of how any physical difficulties impact how we now engage these favored outdoor pastimes. We know that when we are not careful enough and overdo physical activities, we risk injury to ourselves. In frustration we may then think about "hanging it up." But will we too quickly discontinue what we have loved to do because our frustration overwhelms us? Can we find creative ways to still enjoy these pursuits while accepting some degree of physical limitation?

Yet our favored activities are comprised of many layers of experience, beyond what we tend to focus on when we confront only our physical limitations. For example, playing golf probably involves more than shagging a ball around a course for 18 holes. It also involves the camaraderie of friends, the sights, sounds and smells of the course, and the stories of the game we like to talk about afterward.

When our body can't take 18 holes, will we play 9, or 6, or 3? Will we meet a friend or two on the course for an hour or two? Will we enjoy the setting and experience on a very reduced basis without having to hang it up altogether?

Any favored activity includes much more than our physical capacity. Whether golfing, fishing, or gardening, we all will need to make some physical accommodations with time. These favored recreational pursuits include spending time in an activity and setting that we find physically and emotionally nourishing and restorative. And we do this in companionship with others.

As we grow older, we are challenged to make creative and necessary modifications to continue to enjoy what we love to do. Being patient and gentle with ourselves helps us reduce the frustrations associated with whatever physical limitation we may now have. With gentleness and patience we can find ways (and there usually ARE ways) to continue to use our aging bodies in our dance with life: in the garden, on the golf course, on the river, and walking the trail through the woods.

be patient and gentle with our bodies

Chapter Three

Moving on and letting go

Aging changes us. The physical changes that occur in our bodies are not always welcome and sometimes clearly painful and unwanted. But inside our aging bodies we also experience important changes in how we see, think, and feel. We now move into powerfully interesting and valuable transitions in our sense of who we are as persons. These are changes arising through the full ripening of our personality.

This inner transformation associated with our aging propels us toward significant changes in our pattern of living. We are less inclined toward further accumulation of any material possessions and more interested in creating space in our lives for exploring and expressing what is taking shape within us. How will we engage the new challenges and choices that confront us to honor and reflect the fruits of our maturity?

we could remain at home, but should we?

When is it time to move?

For many older people, the answer to that question is a resounding NEVER! They intend to remain in their present home to the very end of life.

As an emblem of independence, remaining at home seems a laudable goal. Knowing this, a broad network of services has been generated over the past decade to facilitate it. We can continue to remain in our home and hire the services we need to support remaining there. Lawn care, snow removal, house cleaning and other related services take away the need to do all we formerly could or wanted to do, assuming we can pay for them. Younger family members might provide some of these services, but may be unfairly burdened by our over-reliance on their time and free labor.

Home health services and transportation services get us to medical appointments or the hospital, pharmacy and grocery store when we need to go there. These help insure that we can "age independently," in our own home.

But, although we could remain at home, should we? What we now refer to as "aging in place" may be a good idea for a time, perhaps a long time, but not for all time. One significant downside to remaining at home for many people is social isolation. As comfortable as home can be, it can also become a lonely place, without regular resource to social connections. Another factor is the time and energy involved in receiving needed care. As we grow older, the coordination required for home based services plus health based services may itself become a strain. Then there's the issue of utility--when there are only two of us, or even one of us, how much space do we need? As we continue to release much of the "stuff" stored around us, probably a whole lot less space than we now have.

When is it time to move? When we can still make the choice. When we can begin to feel the weight of our present circumstances bearing down as the interest in maintaining these circumstances diminishes. When we begin to notice an absence of interesting other people frequenting our lives. When we can imagine a simpler, more engaging, easier and more contented manner of living. Then it's time to seriously consider it.

Downsizing's difficult downside

Growing older brings with it a call to downsize toward a more simple life; a life with fewer objects to care for, less clutter and complication. As we age we want to filter out the stuff we don't need, keeping only what we do, and dispatching the remainder to our adult children or favored charities. Yet even as motivated as we are to reduce our material possessions, how often do we look around our living spaces and wonder why we still have so much stuff? Why do we have such a hard time releasing it?

Indeed, downsizing sounds easier than it often is. Our intention to reduce our storehouse of material goods is often accompanied by a quite understandable reluctance to actually going about accomplishing it. Although we are dealing only with "mere objects," these are often items into which we have placed a significant investment of time, energy and effort. Some are valued possessions that we have repeatedly chosen to keep and have lived with over a long period of time. Some others are repositories for the cherished memories of our family history or reflect a collection of personal life experiences. Some of this "stuff" we have come to love as though it were a part of ourself. We have become "attached."

Whether it's a favorite chair, a classic car, a shotgun or fishing rod or weaving loom or collection of books or musical instrument, some objects have become embedded into the deeper fabric of our life. Some "special" articles of clothing don't go easily out the door to the garage sale, even if only occasionally worn. Some tools reflect the life of a deceased spouse or parent, and carry the "feel" of that cherished person, contributing to our ongoing experience of a no longer living yet still significant and abiding relationship.

Sure, the idea of downsizing, of "letting go" of stuff is simple. But when that stuff is wrapped around our psyche and embedded in our memory, letting go can feel like amputating a small yet important part of ourselves. This turns the simple act of "getting rid of stuff" into a process of releasing pieces of history connected to our very experience of living. It's hard because, while these are "only material things," they are things that have come to matter.

letting go can feel like amputating a part of ourselves...

The discomfort in a new beginning

Starting something new gets easier as we grow older, right? Unfortunately, often not. Attending the first meeting of a new group, or the first day of a class, or meeting someone new, or being exposed to new learning - - for most of us, these "first times" are not particularly enjoyable moments, and our older age and life experience doesn't make them simply disappear. For some of us, starting something new can be so distasteful that nothing "new" rarely ever happens in our lives at all!

Yet our initial awkwardness or apprehension, whether it be about a new friendship or any new activity, must be endured and overcome if we are to continue to learn, grow, and find satisfying relationships. If our discomfort only stops us cold, we are often left to suffer the kind of loneliness and boredom that arises from being stuck with only our past. We have our memories, to be sure, but nothing fresh and alive in our lives in the present time.

While we may be unable to banish entirely our discomfort with a new beginning, we can relate to it differently so it becomes less of a barrier for us. Our discomfort can become a companion that we accept and allow to accompany us as we approach a new situation. Rather than push our discomfort away, we include it without fanfare. When we accept our awkwardness or nervousness at any first time event, other people are usually supportive because they often easily understand that experience from their own lives. Accepting our discomfort helps dissolve its power so we can stay focused on getting what we came to this new situation to find. With a measure of discomfort as our new "friend," we are not pulled off course and can feel more connected and relaxed in this new situation.

Nobody likes to fumble or feel awkward, yet that is very much the price of putting ourselves in any new situation. Even though our discomfort never entirely fades away, we benefit from remembering our own personal history. We remember how we experienced similar discomfort before, and we can recall the learning and friendships that came our way as a result of seeing it through to the other side. And now, taking our discomfort gently by the hand, here we go again.

taking our discomfort gently by the hand...

Even making small choices helps us feel better

We always feel better when we make choices. Being too passive and inactive usually leads only to disappointment and regret, while actively making choices energizes us. It is not the size of the choice but the choosing that matters most.

Even if we are confronted by physical pain or some level of infirmity, the choices we make within each day makes a big difference in how we feel. When we hurt, we need to pay attention to what gives us pleasure. Then we can choose to focus on something we enjoy. When we do that we will notice that although our physical pain may not entirely disappear, it does lose its intensity and we feel better.

Look at the number of small choices we make that work together to bring about what we would, looking back on it, describe as a "pleasant" day. Waking in the morning, we stay attentive to the choices available to us as we consider the day ahead. Rather than becoming a passive victim to whatever befalls us, we make a decision to seek out someone to share a conversation with today. Rather than mindlessly flicking on the TV, we selectively choose what interests us, and decide how long we are willing to watch it. We make a choice to exercise our body, knowing we will feel refreshed afterward. We decide if there is any personal business we need to attend to today, and at least mentally schedule ourselves to do that, to insure that it happens.

These small choices help us feel more alert and active in our life. We know that not everything we want to have happen actually will occur each day. Other people's choices will not always agree with ours. But often they do, and we experience the pleasure of being joined in harmony with them. Also, many of our choices only involve ourselves, so we are free to choose whatever we wish. The small decisions we make about what book to read, or what music we might most enjoy can give us pleasure.

By paying attention to the small choices we are making, we design pleasure and purpose into even an average day. Despite our specific life circumstances or personal struggles, we feel better. It comes through the power of choosing.

we design pleasure and purpose into even an average day

we can release those troublesome expectations

Balanced expectations
for healthy stress

We need some stress to stay healthy, but in just the right amounts. Short term stress can occasionally be helpful. Episodic experiences of stress serve to "prime the pump" and bolster our immune system when the stressor is one we can manage or control. Exercise is an example: we deliberately place our bodies under tension and after tensing up allow our muscles to relax. Moderate exercise is a necessary stressor that enhances our health.

Chronic stress is quite different, particularly when we have little control over the circumstances that generate it. Those of us in care giving roles, taking on the responsibility for the well being of another, are often in this position.

We now know that chronic stress can wear on the cellular structure in our bodies, negatively impacting our immune system and increasing our susceptibility to disease, both physically and mentally. From young soldiers serving in war zones to older adults caring for their spouses, the need to be "on the alert" and responsive to ongoing critical situations exacts its physical and mental toll when carried on over any length of time.

When we carry high expectations about how "things ought to be" we really load the dice on stress. Our expectations can themselves be real stress creators, especially when our expectations are very different from how things actually are. We may, for example, want our adult children and their families to be close and supportive, while they may be spinning in the orbit of their own immediate lives and responsibilities, without us. When we expect to have immediate family around us we can feel abandoned, sad, and lonely with a longing for what right now cannot be.

Unfortunately, if we remain tied to expectations that fail to match our reality, we then likely turn away from what is already available to us: we fail to recognize the close friends who enjoy our company and are actually here with us, (yes, even if they are "not family"). Whenever we build unrealized expectations that are at odds with our real experience, we create a kind of chronic stress that is hauntingly self-perpetuating and unhealthy.

When we release those troublesome expectations we can see what is already here with us. Then we can relax into what we actually have, and enjoy it.

The unwanted poison of bitterness

We are all more health conscious these days. We try to eat right. We exercise. As we grow older we cannot escape the call from every corner to attend closely to each of these ingredients comprising a "healthy lifestyle."

We don't as frequently identify the importance of paying attention to our emotional health. As we understand more about nutrition, we learn to keep certain foods out of our diet because we know they erode our physical health and destroy our energy and vitality. But while we watch what we put into our mouths, we pay less attention to the kinds of feelings we cultivate within us. We can carry destructive feelings around inside that can be every bit as damaging as bad nutrition. Even worse, toxic emotions affect others around us, poisoning their environment as well.

We all know the experience of bitterness and resentment. We remember the venom that could well up inside when life gave us a serious wrong turn. We learned how relationships with others always contained both the sweet and the sour, and have suffered some sour relationships along the way. We noticed that when we held onto sour feelings, we ended up poisoning ourselves. Bitterness and anger darkened our mood and dampened our vitality. These negative feelings clouded our perspective on life and we felt more separate from others and more alone. If we imagined ourselves as plants, we would imagine ourselves noticeably drooping, beginning to wither and die.

We have learned that a sense of withering inside is exactly what happens when we carry bitterness around for very long. As matured and seasoned experiencers of emotion, we desire that our vitality remain undiminished and that joy and delight have space to live inside us. We release the poisonous feelings of bitterness to open space for just such experiences.

Even though our feelings may have been provoked by another person's mean spirited or toxic behavior toward us, we recognize that only we have the power to determine how we will respond to them. It may be hard to do at times, yet when we let go of anger and bitterness, a lightness of mood and buoyancy of spirit results. Life tastes sweeter again, even when nothing has changed on the outside, but something very important has changed inside us.

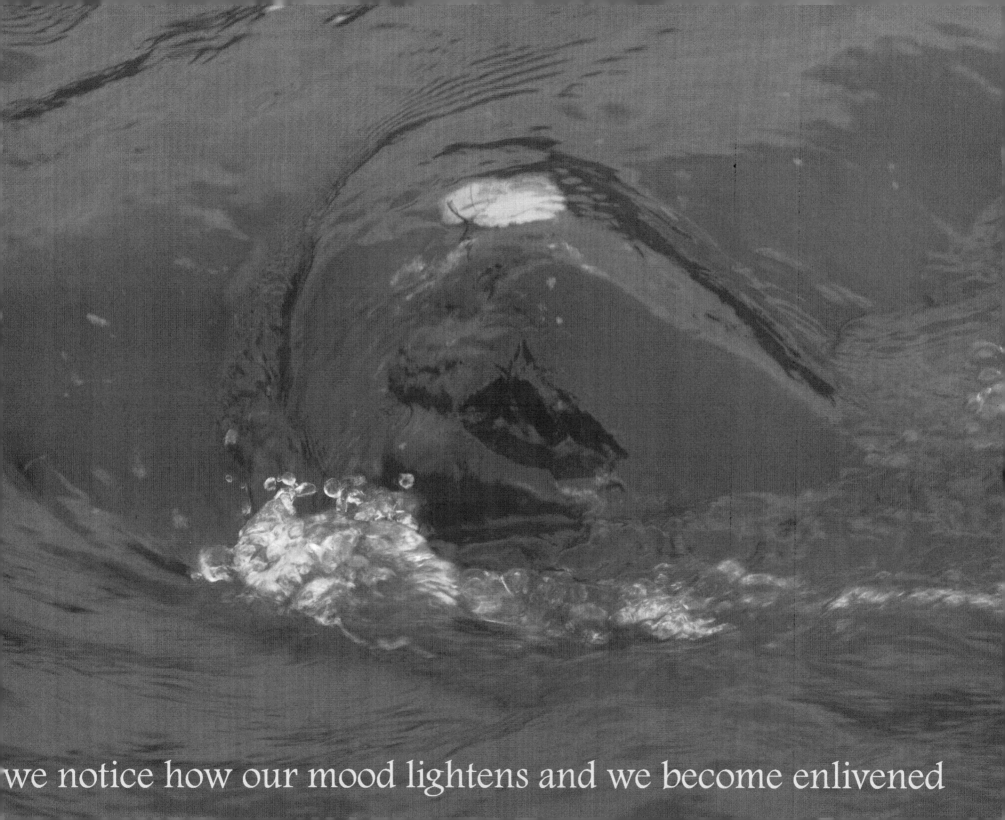

we notice how our mood lightens and we become enlivened

Letting go of regret

Ah, the advantage of age. We can reflect back on our life and more clearly see the effect of the series of choices we have made marking our arrival at this point. At each fork in the road, we chose to take one path and decided against taking another. Yet as we mark our choices through time we may also wonder whether at points we should have chosen differently. Would our lives have been substantially different if we had? Too much of this, however, and we may fall into a pattern of rumination and despair with regret feeling like a stone attached to our soul.

But ruminating about what we did or did not do is also a choice, another path with some unhealthy consequences. Memory alone cannot fully serve to tell us why we, so long ago, made the choices we did. Memory is always selective and over time increasingly spotty and vague. We can easily taint our recall of past choices with criticism or blame. We scold ourselves: we should have known better than chose as we did earlier in our life. Or we tell ourselves that we were ill treated by another, and that's directed our choice.

Regret grows as the "if only's" set in: if only others had treated us better, if only we had been better provided for, if only we had taken another road, if only... We can become paralyzed in these ruminative, looping negative thoughts that add weight to our already heavy feelings. With a steady diet of regret, we live increasingly under a heavy dark cloud. Our vitality is sucked away and our living feels labored. Over time even our physical health is jeopardized. Our immune system flags, more receptive to illness and disease.

Now we can choose to release regret and restore our buoyancy and well being. Right now is a good time, and every day as we make a positive habit of releasing whatever only hurts us when we hold onto it.

Let's make regret "the road not taken." In choosing to release regret we notice how our mood lightens and we become increasingly enlivened as the weight evaporates. Now we are rewarded with energy and vitality. How good it feels to be free!

The power of forgiveness

The power of forgiveness is one of the miracles of human experience. The lives of most older adults contain significant experiences of pain related to injustices created by others. The often quoted truism that "life is not fair" speaks to the injury we suffer that comes our way not of our own doing, but from the hands of others whose actions toward us created harm and wounding. Our parents, spouses, teachers, close friends, even our adult children, can act in ways that hurt and disappoint us. These may deeply affect us and leave large amounts of bitterness and resentment behind. A truly shattering experience that feels like an emotional assault can create an internal sore that continues to bleed, and an experience of pain and anger that continues to gnaw away on the inside.

Forgiveness carries the power to dissolve the poisons that such bitterness and resentment contain. Tightness and constriction in the body find the way to relaxation and release through forgiveness. Our "warmer" emotions like love and compassion are no longer eroded by resentment and anger. The dark shadows of resentment cast over our lives fade with our brightening mood.

Of course, forgiveness is a process that occurs over time. Sometimes it requires the active participation of the person who hurt us, through genuine apology and a request for atonement. Yet even without such an act of contrition by one who has wounded us, we alone have within us the power to offer our forgiveness. We know that forgiveness does not mean forgetting what happened, or the pain it caused. But it always is our choice to forgive regardless of the actions of another.

That's when the miracle begins. We begin to forgive, and we notice almost immediately that we feel more relaxed, responsive, and lively. Our brighter mood is often noticed by others around us. Our capacity to nurture ourselves and others springs back to life. Even elements of despair can turn toward delight and satisfaction in living.

Sometimes we have to work at it, but over time our experience of forgiveness flushes the poison of bitterness and resentment right out of our system. Then compassion and the kind of loving attitude that makes any life worth living has the space it needs to flow through us more easily.

forgiveness is a process...when the miracle begins

Exercise the muscle of compassion

Greater access to compassion is one health benefit available to every older person. Better than prescription medication and free of charge, we receive this benefit by committing to a regular pattern of exercise with compassion.

We can roughly define compassion as our ability to carefully attend to the experience of another person in a supportive way. We feel "with" them, and want to understand what they might be experiencing. We know what it's like to be on the receiving end of someone's compassion toward us. We usually sense this as a warm, calm and relaxed feeling that accompanies the kindness, gentleness, and understanding offered us by another. It has the impact of a beneficial drug, and can be felt as a genuinely "mood altering" experience. Because it is such a positive experience that we older adults access easily, we tend also to notice it more easily in other people and want to be around them or seek them out when we're troubled or feeling down.

If acting compassionately is such powerful medicine with good results, why aren't we using more of it? Some days we may not feel up to as much as saying "hello" to the neighbor next door. We may be tired, or preoccupied with something worrying us, or just "off our game" in some way. These are the very times that we need a more muscular capacity to deliver a compassionate response. If we have exercised compassion regularly, and made a habit of kindness and understanding, we can more easily break through our own sour mood to reach out to a neighbor, friend, even a stranger, at those times when it's more difficult. When our compassionate response doesn't depend upon our being in a good mood, and we have enough muscle behind our compassion, we can more often be our better selves even at troubled times. We can break through our reluctance and show compassion even when it isn't easy to do so.

When we are able to show up with compassion, we notice that something really interesting happens inside us. We feel better and livelier. Compassion offered to another always bounces back to the one who gives it. A powerful medicine with healing properties for sender and receiver alike, compassion carries beneficial side effects for everyone.

compassion bounces back to the one who gives it

We find happiness exercising appreciation

A good deal of energy, time and money is drained away in various attempts to insure our happiness. Most often, we are encouraged to look outside ourselves to find happiness in a world of objects and other people. We will be happy if we are able to buy this or that new shiny object. Or, if we can get the right people to like us, then we will be happy.

Alas, there is some kernel of truth in this when we are young. The new toy does deliver pleasure for a short while. Being liked by someone we want to like us does increase our happiness for a time. But after awhile, what was shiny and new becomes only ordinary, and we need to find the next best thing or the next best person to help us feel better. As we grow older, we begin to figure out that any source of happiness invested outside ourselves will be fleeting. Getting someone to like us, or finding something new to buy, we learn, will bring at best only short lived pleasure.

Happiness, we discover sometimes slowly and sometimes as a sudden "aha" revelation, is actually a capacity we carry inside ourselves, not something we can reach for and grab like the brass ring on a merry-go-round. We learn that happiness is a direct consequence of practicing appreciation. Indeed, as we mature, we find the exercise of appreciation to be our most reliable avenue to any lasting experience of happiness.

There is tremendous relief and great freedom in noticing how easy this can be. Increasingly we appreciate the "small wonders" of the world that surround us every day. The kindness of ordinary people fills us with pleasure when we take the time to notice and experience it. The bounty of nature, with flowers and bird song, become something more worthy of our attention. Meanness in people doesn't interest us because it destroys our experience of happiness. Even the simplest of objects, carefully chosen, give us more pleasure than stuff that looks attractive but only clutters up our life.

Interested in increasing your experience of happiness? Look first at the daily practice of exercising appreciation. That is the true "royal road" to any real and lasting experience of happiness.

the "small wonders" of the world surround us

we release how things "ought to be"

A grateful heart

We get older and settle into a certain rhythm of living. But just when we imagine ourselves to finally "have it all together," something arises to poke a hole in our contentment. Our children, now all launched into their own lives, sail into the rocks and struggle rather than peacefully moving across a calm horizon. Or a health concern surfaces, or our finances begin to unravel. Or the global tension dominating the evening news is disturbing and pulls at our attention.

But the process of aging and the life experience purchased over time demonstrates a persistent realization: the outer circumstances of our lives ultimately do not determine our inner attitude. From the shape of the economy to the health and well being of our children, we are always influenced and affected by factors beyond our power to control. These will impact our mood and influence our experience. Yet, however great their force in our life, they do not ultimately dictate what we experience within ourselves. That power continues to reside in the subjective, interior realm of our being, held deeply inside.

That is the power of the heart. Indeed, we often hear that a grateful heart is the cornerstone of contentment as we grow older. Our heart's gratitude has little to do with having the exterior and more visible aspects of our lives closely mirror our expectations of how things "ought to be." Rather, our experience of gratitude more likely arises when we release whatever pre-existing expectations we carry within us.

Accepting the circumstances of our outer reality does not mean that we like them or want them to continue. We may decide to use our energy and intellect to make useful and constructive "outside" changes whenever we can do so. But we will not allow these exterior circumstances to rob us of the joy that is also present in our midst: in our friendships and in the other "loves" in our lives (of nature, music, art, literature, etc.). A grateful heart knows that our life is always larger than any particular life situation that brings us pain. We may have regret or disappointment or concern about any of the realities we confront, but these do not erase gratitude so much as they season and flavor our experience of life.

Chapter Four

Creating a new path

The emerging landscape of aging is an entirely new territory for each of us who have been privileged to travel beyond the more constricting confines of adulthood. We have worked to pare away many of the false beliefs that would inhibit our travel into this new horizon, and we have rendered asunder much of the trappings of perhaps formerly useful but now limiting past identities, activities, and associations.

Now we are ready to take further steps and forge a pathway into a deeper experience of our own unique and individual life as an older adult. The "gifts" of age help guide our footsteps here. We can count on our broadened perspective, our deeper in-visioning, our enhanced courage and compassion. Our challenge is to become more fully ourselves while developing meaningful relationships with other older unique selves whose path joins ours. Age has opened this opportunity while this "harvest of maturity" grants us the capacities that make this journey possible.

how do we relate to mystery

In life's mystery, where shall we place our expectations?

Significant aspects our our lives lie always shrouded in mystery. Even in these older years, none of us are able to foretell the unknown influences that will impact our lives right through to life's end. We can never know what potential opportunities for friendship, love, or learning are right at the as yet unseen edge of our existence.

How do we relate to mystery? The process of contemplating any new beginning, be it an activity or whole new phase of living, is also a good time to tune in to our relationship with expectations and uncertainty within our own life. Since disappointment is the other side of expectation, we can also more clearly identify our expectations by taking a measure of our disappointments.

It is a truism to state that many of our expectations are, and have been, thwarted through time. We expect that life will continue in a predictable pattern, until suddenly, it doesn't. Then the positive anticipation, eager excitement, or just plain comfortable companionability that we experienced before is replaced by pain and disappointment. Our health may change or our friends or children may move far away. And how do we prepare ourselves for the death of a loved one; of course we are shocked when that suddenly occurs and our life is diminished by loss. Changing circumstance may be something we imagined happening to someone else, but then it happens to us and we are hurt and dismayed.

When smashing disappointment occurs, where do we then place our expectations? Do we now attach expectation directly to disappointment, and expect that from here on only disappointment will befall us? Clearly, this can be a tempting form of self protection, just to avoid more hurt later on. But doing so is also an avoidance of the mystery that life (and "reality") actually is! When we expect disappointment we risk foreclosing on the as yet unrealized possibilities that lie before us, at any age.

One of the great advantages of healthy aging is an ease in living with this uncertainty. It is we older adults who are best able to reach beyond life's inevitable disappointments into the surrounding unknown, and prosper from the new relationships and new learning that our explorations reveal.

Too old to begin something new?

"I'd like to learn another language, but I'm afraid I'm too old to start something that complicated" says the 65, 75 or 80 year old who now has time for something he or she may have long wanted to do. Or, "I'd like to learn to play an instrument, but I'm afraid I no longer have the dexterity or fine motor coordination I'd need for that" says another. In each case, age is used as a stop sign, a barrier constructed against starting something new.

A danger lurks here. When we close the door to new learning, we cut ourselves off from the source of our own vitality. Older years become a time of stasis and stagnation as we turn away from our passions and neglect our connection with our inner creativity and continuing desire for growth. Then we starve our brains of the stimulation required to keep us mentally robust and physically and emotionally vibrant. Physical and mental health take their toll as a result.

Continued growth and maturity resides within our DNA. We are vital and energetic older adults capable of forming our creative urges into interesting and challenging new adventures. We know to be realistic about these, and set our sights about our new pursuits accordingly. We set the bar too low when guided by an "I'm too old" message. We set the bar too high if we permit perfection to turn exciting new learning into a burdensome experience. Perfect fluency in a new language will not be our goal, but rather using it "well enough" for our purpose, for travel, conversation, even reading. We strive not to play an instrument at a high quality, professional level but rather to enjoy our new skill with our family, friends, and perhaps even other older musicians (catching the edge of the "senior garage band" phenomenon). Our ability to do something today that we couldn't do yesterday is personally rewarding and sufficiently motivating to keep us stimulated, challenged, and excited about our life.

We confront seemingly endless choices about what new learning we will undertake. Whatever form we choose to engage will nurtures our lives and fuel our bodies and brains. We mark these older years with continuing growth and on-going vitality, and make our lives examples for those that follow.

continued growth and vitality resides within our DNA

Our quest for beauty grows stronger

In Plato's philosophy, beauty was directly linked to divinity. Our quest for finding beauty in our lives was, at essence, a way of experiencing God. This quest, present in all human beings, only intensifies with age.

As we grow older we become less distracted by superficial glitter, and trade in quantity for quality in our search for the beautiful. A smaller number of deep friendships are now much more appealing than a wide network of acquaintances. We sort through material possessions, filtering out the many and choosing to keep only those we regard as significant.

Some of us may more formally "study beauty," by taking the classes increasingly available to older people where we learn to paint, play an instrument or write poetry. More often our search for beauty seems like a treasure hunt, a "search for the really valuable" that we conduct amidst the ordinary activities of our everyday living.

Our personal descriptions of what we find to be beautiful can be as unique and individual as are each of us. We find beauty in flowers and paintings and sunsets, but also in the classic design of some automobiles, or some bridges, or in the architecture of some buildings. We find beauty in the face of another person, in the shape of the human body, in the sloppy grin of the family dog and the ripples from the wind caressing the river. We catch an edge of what is beautiful and know it when we experience it because it inspires us and "lifts us up." Beauty nourishes us, and we easily want more of it.

Those who research the psychic landscape inhabited by older adults claim that honing in on and refining our experience of beauty is one of the principle occupations of this stage of life. There is in this claim much to encourage and gratify us. We older adults have learned to be sensitive to the underlying values guiding our choices about how we will spend our time, attention, energy and resources. We've been around the block a few times by now, and we know how to tell what has real value from what only sucks up our energy and wastes our time. We aren't about to settle for cheap imitations when we've developed a nose for the real thing!

we trade in quantity for quality in our search for the beautiful

Aging's call to creativity

Older people are increasingly recognized as bundles of creativity. Notice the recent explosion of arts programs for seniors regionally and across the country. Today entire older adult communities centered around various expressions of creativity are being developed. Painting, writing, music, crafts and the domestic arts like quilting, woodworking, cooking and baking; the theme highlighting creativity in older persons abounds.

Why does the thrust of creative energy push so insistently at older ages? Is it just having the time and resources after work life and child rearing are much less demanding? Is creative expression only another form of puttering around to fill up otherwise empty days?

This may be the case for some, but the core truth is decidedly different. The very process of aging brings with it an upturn in our creative juices. When we look deeply into any ordinary life, we find beneath the surface the residue from a number of unformed possibilities that were not or could not be developed earlier. All of us have other selves within —possible other expressions of our being that we could have nurtured had we made other choices at earlier points in our lives. But we chose what we did, and pushed aside other possibilities.

Some of these "undeveloped selves" may remain alive within us today, the root of some latent talent pressing for our energy and attention. These are unexpressed potentialities that clamor to occupy some of the space freed up through the change in life tasks and responsibilities that older age allows.

We may be tempted to say that it is now far too late for this kind of foolishness, that our past choices are now simply locked behind us. But are they? Look at the displays of creativity spiraling around almost any community where you live. And take a second look at what you experience when you explore your own untapped inner sources of energy and vitality.

The process of aging favors self knowledge, confidence, and a diminished concern about the judgment and approval of others. The creative muse, in whatever form, is free to emerge in our older years precisely because we seem more psychologically attuned and available. Now we can choose to pay attention to what we had earlier put away. But will we?

the creative muse is free to emerge

Encouraging the spirit of adventure

As children, the spirit of excitement and adventure is our native tongue. We want to dig into life and explore the world around us. We do that through early fantasy play, constructing epic adventures in which spaces in our houses are remade into castles or forts, and our backyards become wilderness, or kingdoms in foreign lands in other times. Growing older, we branch out, taking our explorations into the neighborhood with friends.

Now that we are many decades on the far side of childhood, where is the "spirit of adventure" that was so central to our experience in those younger days? Does the adventurous spirit necessarily fade with age?

Not at all, as many examples of the adventurous lives of older people continue to testify. In fact, one national resource, the Growing Bolder Media Group, has amassed an extensive series of profiles of adventurous and even thrill seeking older adults continuing their remarkable exploits well into their 90's. (These are available for your on-line viewing at GrowingBolder.com).

One such senior adventurer who thought deeply about the importance of keeping this spirit alive and kicking was "Granny" Haddock. Granny, who died not long ago in New Hampshire at age 100, was well known as a political activist who came into her activism later in her life. She was 89 years old when she walked across the country to promote campaign finance reform. That "adventure" set the stage for her next one: she ran for the U.S. Senate at age 94.

Granny was well aware of nourishing the spirit of adventure within herself in her later life and allowing it to flourish in areas that interested and excited her. In addition to her social activism, she was a writer, and offered her readers the following advice:

> "You have to keep the young adventurer inside your heart alive long enough for it to someday reemerge. It may take some coaxing and some courage, but that person is in you always, never growing old."

Granny had it right! The spirit of the young adventurer lives in the hearts of us all. Whether through later life social activism, engagement with the creative arts, or the thrill of new friendships and new learning, our "young adventurer" strives always to reemerge.

keep the young adventurer inside your heart alive

A time designed
for spiritual growth

Looking for spiritual growth opportunities? Then look at your life right now because in the life of any older adult, these are abundantly available.

Contemporary culture has been infected with an array of confusing spiritually oriented books and related media programs. Most of these suggest that you should be doing something you're probably not doing, or know something you're told you don't already know, or travel somewhere exotic, or buy something (almost always it's buying something). You might well scratch your head and ask: "Is any of this really necessary?"

We oldsters who have explored many of these suggested approaches, traditions, and materials, advise caution here. Why? Because the most interesting and exciting recent studies in aging suggests that "spiritual growth," defined as someone growing in compassion, generosity, tolerance, graciousness, and depth of understanding, arises directly from the experience of healthy aging! Spiritual retreats can be helpful, as can reading some materials, or participating in some communities. But the most important ingredient on the spiritual path, we increasingly find, is paying careful attention to our own life. We carefully observe how we regard and treat the people around us. We reflect on the attitudes and values we demonstrate in our interactions with others. These attitudes and perspectives promoting compassion, graciousness, etc., are enhanced through the conscious process of healthy aging.

Everyone with some wear on their tires already well knows that it isn't what you say about what you believe that matters near so much as how you "walk the talk" through your actions. It's in the doing, in people being kind to each other, helping and caring for each other, where the heart and soul of any "Spiritual Growth" program lies. Spiritual growth is reflected in our pattern of daily living, and visible to us whenever we look carefully at the kind of behavioral trail we leave in our relationships, and in choices we make to be of service to others.

Buy the book or sign up for the "spiritual growth opportunity" if you choose to, but let's keep a clear headed perspective about it. Our unfolding life through this aging process offers plenty of opportunity for spiritual growth. If we pay attention to how we live, love, and engage in the world, we can observe daily the fruits of these opportunities.

growing spiritually is paying attention to our own life

Our amazing older brain

Almost every day we discover more about how our brains actually work. Much of our new knowledge comes from advanced technology that, for the first time, allows us to "see into" the workings of our brain. This helps us ask better questions that guide our understanding of how our brains continue to change as we age.

Before we had access to this modern technology, our best brain science models suggested that our brains were fixed ("hard wired" we might now say) after the first few years of life. Later, we came to learn that our brain was more plastic than we had realized, and that one part of our brain could compensate for another part when necessary. This was what happened when, for example, a person suffered a stroke that affected the part of the brain that controlled their capacity to speak or walk, and the control of those necessary functions would be taken over by another part. Our brains, we learned, were far more plastic and less fixed than we had supposed.

Now we've taken another step in our knowledge about how our brains function. We are learning that our brains continue to develop throughout our lives. We see how ongoing neural growth facilitates the "mature thinking" that makes older brains more complex, and recognize how important new learning is to the health of our brain. To stay healthy, our older brain requires exercise just as much as our body does.

What is a good exercise regimen for our brain? As with our body, stretching is important. What stretches our brain? Exploring something new, different from the ordinariness of everyday life does that. Adding a new skill or ability, or working to refine and further develop something we more superficially know also stretches our brain.

Physical exercise also involves building and maintaining strength and endurance. Mental exercise is similar. Those that strengthen our brain engage cognitive tasks that carry some minimal level of difficulty. A lazy, always comfortable, brain routine turns out not to be a healthy one over time. Our brains need to be stimulated and working to learn to stay healthy. It could be about music, gardening, dancing or philosophizing. If the activities we choose stimulate, excite and challenge us, our brains are receiving the exercise necessary for continuing good health.

"mature thinking" makes older brains more complete

Where's my tribe?

Our human brains and hearts may look very similar from a biological perspective, but inside our brains and hearts we are quite individual and unique. Our experience of what excites our passions and drives our curiosity may be very different within any group of maturing older people. The kind of social environment in which we feel comfortable in pursuing our unique interests and passions may also be quite distinct. Not all guys care about NFL football, for example, although many do. Not everyone, female or male, wants to talk about philosophy, cooking, or gardening either. Then, too, some of us prefer a close, more intimate setting for important conversations, while others of us care less about that and are comfortable conversing in larger social settings.

These individual distinctions in our interests and passions, and the differing kinds of social environments we choose to pursue them, present us with both struggles and opportunities as we age. While our need for intellectual and social stimulation is as great as it ever was, we have to find new ways of "feeding" them. Formerly established work or school related social networks are gone. Now we often have to rely on our own initiative to search out important continuing sources of social and intellectual nourishment.

Finding these sources is often not an easy task. When our interests and passions diverge from most others it takes a greater effort to search out and locate the "tribe" of those who do share them. We want to take on this task with a light heart, seeking "compatible souls" who affirm and share in our particular curiosities and possibly idiosyncratic activities. Our dedication to our search for like-minded others helps us break through any experience of social isolation and alienation we might otherwise feel. Finding our "tribe" rewards and energizes us. It dissolves any sense we might have that our particular expression of individuality was evidence of some kind of personal defect.

Relationships that stimulate our curiosity and feed our soul require our commitment and active support. We are encouraged in the knowledge that there are others as yet unknown to us who also find nourishment in what nourishes us. Bringing these valuable connections into full blown reality is one of the important challenges associated with healthy aging.

"compatible souls" who affirm and share our curiosities

Chapter Five

We care about quality in relationships

Healthy older adults have a deep and abiding concern about the quality of their relationships with those who reside in their circle of care. In fact, placing a primary value on high quality relationships is one of the most significant changes associated with the process of aging. Quality trumps quantity as we easily sacrifice a slew of more superficial acquaintances for a handful of truly deep and meaningful friendships.

Age has ripened us, honing our capacity to be more fully present, to attend and listen more deeply, and to speak more directly from our heart. Indeed, the richness we experience in relationship is one of aging's most precious rewards.

Love changes as we grow older

An older man had recently become a widower. Reflecting on the loss of his spouse, he mused openly, "what does anyone really know about love?" His thoughtful tone suggested that this was a question he had been pondering for some time. His probing exploration revealed a keen awareness about how the experience of love, and of loving, changes as we age. It's often said that we "grow in love" as we grow older, but that only seems to capture something rather abstract about his process. A maturing experience of love through the process of aging comprises much more.

The poet and all-around wise woman, May Sarton, wrote years ago about the maturing nature of love. She called her piece "Lighter With Age," and is repeated below.

> "Love, we still think, many of us, is for the young. But what do they really know about it? It is hard for them to differentiate between sexual passion and love itself, for instance.
>
> If the whole of life is a journey toward old age, then I believe it is also a journey toward love. And love may be as intense in old age as it was in youth, only it is different, set in a wider arc, and the more precious because the time we have to enjoy it is bound to be brief.
>
> Old age is not a fixed point, any more than sunrise or sunset or the ocean tide. At every instant the psyche is in flux: 'And like a newborn spirit did he pass/Through the green evening quiet in the sun,' as Keats put it.
>
> Whether on the edge or in the very center of old age, Sarton continues, "we sense we may be 'new-born spirits' at any moment, if we have courage. Old age is not an illness, it is a timeless ascent. As power diminishes, we grow toward more light."

Sarton says a mouthful here. And Einstein, (who doesn't like to evoke his name on any topic?) in his older years, said that love was the glue that held the universe together. Doesn't love also help us hold our individual lives together in much the same way? As we mature in love, we become whole people who carry more light because we are more loving. That is a gift of healthy aging.

Giving the gift of attention

How rare a gift this is. The true value of genuine attention paid to another person can be measured by noting how uncommon it is and how infrequently we experience it. Attention is the gold in any relationship, and just like gold, is both rare and precious.

Often confused with something more superficial, real attention can be defined by what it is not. Attention is not a glance and nod, a handshake and a "how you doin'?" It is also not the stare into the middle distance with half an ear into a conversation. And it most definitely is not the construction of a laundry list of tasks to attend to while pretending to be engaged in listening to someone.

Real attention means "being there," present and available to another person without distraction. To pay attention is to focus on the other with a keen interest and curiosity about their life, with no other agenda operating in that moment. Attention means pausing to take the time to actually see the unique life of the other person. This kind of attention cannot be hurried. Making time and space in your life for someone else, to "be there" without distraction, are the primary components of real attention.

Paying this kind of attention to another person is a demonstration of love, and in modern times probably one of the most rare of gifts we have to give. Living in an electronic age with the clatter of mobile phones, computers, and TV's, we have grown quite familiar with forms of "communication" that only serve to separate us from any sense of genuine human connection. Electronic "attention" we know from experience, is attention divided between multiple interactions, sometimes on multiple devices, even among multiple people.

In today's fast paced society, everyone is at risk of being swept up into scattered and divided "non-attention." Because we older adults carry memories of the gifts of attention we have received from those who cherished us along the way, we know its power and necessity. We have learned that paying careful attention to someone is a clear indication of our love, care and interest in them. Of the gifts we remember, the memory of being "attended to," clearly and without distraction, carries special prominence.

paying attention is a demonstration of love

children draw emotional support from significant elders

We influence other generations

If we are occasionally given to wonder whether and how much older people might matter in the lives of others, we can be encouraged by recent reports that illustrate the important role we play in the personality development of younger ones. We've long known that relationships with grandparents were important to the development of children. What we didn't know was how powerfully relationships with older adults also positively impact their now middle aged adult children.

In a youth oriented culture such as ours has been, older adults don't get regular reminders of their value to society's younger members. The picture portrayed by studies on personality development is strong and compelling. Relationships with grandparents are significant sources of healing for the multiple numbers of children struggling with issues related to emotional security and stability. In addition, the adult children of older people also continue to draw emotional support from parents and other significant elders in their lives.

When we recognize that most kids get bumped around and bruised through the "normal" course of growing up, a good relationship with a healthy grandparent is a source of nurturance and healing for just about any child. Yet the benefit of a relationship with an older person goes further. Personality development continues throughout the lifespan, and doesn't stop at childhood or adolescence as we once thought. Recognizing this, we see that our adult children are also on a trajectory of continued development, and not surprisingly, at times turn to their elders (parents, uncles, aunts, older friends) as a significant emotional resource when they hit their own "bumps in the road."

What quality or characteristics do we older people have that has such profound value to those in relationship with us? Most striking is our capacity to provide an uncritical interest and acceptance of loved ones who live in these younger generations. This kind of emotional maturity and capacity for nurturance that makes acceptance possible becomes more available through healthy aging. We have just what so many others want and need!

We are potential sources of emotional healing through our relationships. As older adults, we make a particularly profound and lasting difference when we extend our care into the lives of others.

We celebrate our greater capacity for the gift of friendship

We can be friendly with people for free, but real friendship is pricier. The true cost of friendship, of the time, energy and investment in knowing and caring about another person, is one which people say they are strongly interested in and much more willing to pay as they grow older.

As we age we become increasingly built for relationships. We now possess a greater depth of experience, have garnered more emotional maturity and stability, and express more social competence than most younger adults can manage. Our desire for deeper and more substantial friendships comes with an increased capacity to make those kind of relationships possible. We might say, on the good authority of our own experience, that a heightened capacity for friendship is one of the most beneficial "fruits of aging."

We cannot fail to notice how frequently this quest for depth of connection shows itself in the lives of elders. Asked about what they might want as a birthday or holiday gift, how many older people exclaim, "I want time with my friends, with my family, with people I love." We learn to recognize "the gift of time" as the most valuable one we can offer each other, far more precious than the store bought substitutes that only distract us and leave us too often feeling empty and alone.

As older adults, we have lived through a long period of adulthood during much of which the quantity of time available to us seemed scarce. Time was too often divided among a variety of important responsibilities. These multiple pulls on our time made it more difficult to be "all in one place," and to feel genuinely available, even when we were with a cherished friend.

Now, in the older years that allow us to cast off the chains of adulthood, we live in a more evolved and less distracted phase of our life. We are blessed with the advanced emotional maturity and enhanced perspective about the truly important things in life that comes with age. We know the value of sharing time with someone as an expression of caring and being cared for in return. These are the great gifts we bring to life in our mutual expressions of friendship.

we know the value of sharing time as an expression of caring

effective communication ~ a smile and simple, kind words

Word power:
The simplest gift

Years ago a colleague and I were leading a workshop on learning to communicate effectively. During a break, one of the participants, an elderly man spoke with me. He said he thought what we were trying to teach was quite important. But the most important kind of communication was really much simpler than we made it. Then he backed his statement up with this story.

He said his wife had died a couple of years before, following a lengthy illness. He was devastated by her death, and went into a "deep funk" that lasted a long time. He didn't go out of his house except for a rare trip to the store, didn't call his friends or his children, and didn't answer the phone when anyone called him. "I just didn't really care about anything," he said. "I thought my friends and my kids had taken on the job of trying to cheer me up, and I didn't want anything to do with any of that."

After months of keeping his pain locked up inside, he allowed himself a small shopping trip to get a few necessities. "I was just walking down the street, feeling miserable and looking down at my shoes as I went, when suddenly I heard a woman's voice say 'good morning'. It was a kind, happy voice, and I looked up because I didn't know if she was talking to me. But she was – an old lady, about my old man age, just noticing me and smiling. I felt like I couldn't help myself- - I just smiled back and said 'hello.'"

That made a strong impact on him. He started to look around him and not just at the ground, and greeted a few other people on the street. When he got back home, he noticed that he felt better. He even answered his phone that night, and agreed to attend a church service with one of his kids the next Sunday.

"The funny thing is," he told me, "I have no idea who that woman was. I only know that she noticed me and greeted me simply and kindly." That, he told me, was what effective communication was; a smile, and simple, kind words that could help take away the hidden pain in another person's life, even when spoken by a stranger.

Aging means inevitable loss

How often we hear older people talk about how hard it is to watch friends die off around them. They even describe being afraid to answer the phone for fear of more bad news at the other end of the line.

These are inevitable experiences for older people. Living a long life brings with it the experience of multiple significant losses, including possibly a spouse and siblings, in addition to cherished old friends. Indeed, in older age life turns increasingly from weddings to funerals—from occasions of celebration to occasions for grieving.

No one likes losing people they care about. Each time we lose someone we love we want to rail against our powerlessness to do anything about the loss. Our anguished protest helps us release some of the anger and powerlessness we feel, and relieves our pent up emotion. We're still sad, but calmer and now more in touch with what the person we lost actually meant to us. Then the process of healing this new wound can begin.

Any significant loss is an assault to our psyche. We are cut open, and want to withdraw and lick our wounds. We feel deeply hurt, and may respond to our pain by avoiding any painful reminders of the one we lost, like avoiding familiar places where we had often spent time together, or the activities we enjoyed. We may also want to isolate ourselves from future painful losses by avoiding contact with people because we anticipate losing them too, including family and friends. We shut down our relationships to protect ourselves.

Yet following significant loss we need other people to help us heal. Reaching out is particularly hard when we are so tempted to withdraw. We may notice how the process of healing our emotional wounds is very similar to healing wounds to our bodies. Remember back when we were told it was better to expose a clean wound to the open air than to cover it with a bandage? Our inside wounds caused by having someone important to us ripped out of our life also heal best when we expose them to the atmosphere of friends and family. We heal better when we let others see our sorrow, and when we allow our tears to more freely cleanse our wounds.

significant loss is an assault…we want to withdraw and lick our wounds

we are in daily contact with the roots of our relationship

Death does not end a relationship

The death of someone we love changes everything in ways profound and shattering. Our world is turned upside down, and something that has been a solid anchor in our lives is shorn away. The grief and sadness associated with such a loss is beyond measure.

But our experience of relationship with the person who has died does not end in their death. We have invested our heart, our time and our energy, often through decades, in warming into the life of another who we have grown to love. Their life, dear friend or spouse, has taken root in us and become intertwined with the roots of our own life. Death cuts down the figure towering above ground, but death does not destroy the entangling root system growing beneath.

With death comes the ending of the active and ordinary everyday engagement with the physical form and appearance of our beloved other. There is no person to see, to talk with, to touch or hold. But these deep interwoven memories remain wrapped around our life. With long and layered histories together, our connection in relationship has filtered into our bones and blood. We are in daily contact with the roots of our relationship with the one we have lost.

How do we now relate to this person no longer physically present, but alive in our consciousness? We need to shun the advice of those well meaning "helpers" who encourage us to "get over" our experience of loss, because we know that "getting on with our lives" means being in a relationship that continues inside us. Now we have to live that relationship differently. We communicate differently. We continue conversations that were well rehearsed over our many years together. We listen carefully for the voice of the departed that continues to sound inside us, sometimes wistfully reminding us about elements of our common history, sometimes humorously poking our feeble but necessary efforts to cope with their physical loss.

Being human means that loving relationships are always essential to our continuing well-being. When such a relationship is disrupted through death, and only one life continues while another fades from exterior view, the root connection remains. This connection nurtures and supports us through our grief, and into our continuing life beyond.

Loneliness finds a cure in genuine friendship

Oh, the multiple ways loneliness can creep into our lives as we age, and ravage the very foundation of our health. The extreme consequences laid at the doorstep of loneliness have been the subject of considerable research in recent years and have helped us better understand just how devastating an impact it has on our mental, emotional and physical health. Singled out among other maladies associated with aging, loneliness has been declared a significant "silent killer" among older adults.

Doubtless, most of us have known something of the experience of loneliness within our own lives. Out of those experiences, we have learned to distinguish being alone from being lonely. We know that being alone can feel just fine, even be at times a welcome and refreshing nourishment for us, while being lonely feels only painful and debilitating.

Even more painful is the invisible loneliness that we experience when other people are physically present around us, but relate only in an emotionally disconnected way. Feeling isolated in those situations where we expect to find warmth and closeness are occasions of the most intense experiences of loneliness. We can find painful loneliness within a marriage or even within our family. Acute loneliness can persist within other forms of relationships as well. Sometimes so-called "friendships" are actually between people who are deeply lonely. In any of these situations, older adults who appear well connected in relationships may suffer the misery of loneliness entirely invisible to an outsider's eye.

We only perpetuate our experience of loneliness when we isolate from others and fail to acknowledge our feeling. Yet, the emotional pain associated with continuing loneliness wears heavily on our body, and extracts a terrible toll on our health.

However we have come to loneliness, we find its cure in genuine friendship. Here we create a relationship of respect, care and mutual concern. Within this safe environment we build an emotional closeness that doesn't happen quickly, but arrives through time and experience. We learn to speak from our heart while carefully listening to the heart of the other. We come to know ourselves as vulnerable human beings who have chosen to jointly become the very "medicine" that heals this affliction.

we learn to speak from our heart while carefully listening

When love seems far away

Many of us carry images of the "Hallmark Card" close-knit family around a tree or the family dinner table at holiday times. When we compare that image to what lies immediately before us in our own lives, our personal circumstance can appear bleak and impoverished. Our own families may be scattered around the country, even the world. Many of our most cherished friends may now be deceased or have moved away, and we are alone.

When this is our reality, so different than the fabulous pictures of holiday cheer presented to us by the media, we can feel not just alone, but lonely indeed. Now the holiday season hangs over us like a wet blanket, something to be dreaded rather than celebrated, to be "gotten over with" rather than enjoyed. The tendency to isolate ourselves within our loneliness is strong.

But another reality also surrounds us, one just as real as our distance from friends and family, just as real as the death of those we loved, once close to us and now gone. This is the stark reality of the lives lived by others in the community around us. They, if they are of any significant age, have also suffered and are suffering the absence of loving connection by death and distance. All of us who have walked through miles of living have suffered separation from those we love. When we look around us at others in our community, we are looking at the faces of individuals who have experienced profound loss, and now possibly profound loneliness.

How will we now connect with those who are our neighbors, and whose "Hallmark Card" family is just as fractured as our own? Will we greet them warmly rather than shy away? Will we risk sharing a meal with them? Will we express an interest in their lives, just as we would want others to express an interest in ours?

Any of the "Hallmark Holiday" times of the year are heralded as "seasons of giving." Giving gifts of love may look like a kind word, a conversation, or an invitation to a meal. These are simple gifts borne out of our human need for loving connection. When this gift is given, and received, love no longer feels so far away.

holiday season hangs over us like a wet blanket

"A Christmas Carol" – A morality play for older folks

Remember Charles Dickens' "A Christmas Carol"? Three spirits present themselves to the aging, embittered and cynical Scrooge: the ghosts of Christmas past, present, and yet to come speak to him about the consequences of his miserly and dispirited life. We older adults know the truth of Dickens' story. We have long learned to recognize generosity or stinginess in the spirit and attitudes of people around us, and we know how much these can affect us.

"Bah humbug" is an expression of a stingy and sour attitude toward others that is usually an attempt to avoid the emotional pain associated with the fear of rejection. Each of us knows this fear, and find in ourselves both a lively and generous spirit and one more protective ("bah humbug"), hunkered down and withdrawn. Into this internal emotional mixture we must add the impact that outer events (the "news of the day") have on our mood and subjective sense of well being. Then, like Scrooge, we must be careful lest the volatile combination of external issues rubbing against our own inner fears leak out to contaminate our attitude and poison our relationships.

For Ebenezer Scrooge it was the ghost of Christmas yet to come that shocked him out of his protective isolation, his "bah humbug" suit of armor. Scrooge was confronted by the impact his attitude had on others, how his embittered past and fear of emotional pain affected the lives of everyone whose life touched his. Dickens tale has Scrooge finally recognize his power to change and choose differently. When he "gets it," the compassion that lay hidden beneath his protective, miserly exterior is fully resurrected, and the play ends with an outpouring of love and joy all around.

We "get it" too. Dickens' "A Christmas Carol" is a morality play for any older person. It invites us to more fully understand that, in spite of what we have experienced from the past, our present attitude affects the lives of others, children or adults, in profound ways. Like Ebenezer Scrooge, we can choose to emphasize the bitterness and cynicism that we carry protectively within ourselves, or reach beneath it toward a more generous spirit of love and compassion. At any season, the door is open for either. The choice is ours.

our present attitude affects the lives of others in profound ways

Chapter Six

Reflecting our value as elders

Aging is not a simple nor an easy journey. We have often been misperceived and our value under-appreciated. Looking at the world around us, we see that this is changing, and we see, too, that those who have recently gone before us and those who journey now alongside us are the very agents of that change.

People have begun to view aging differently, in large measure because we have shown them a larger picture of our older years that they have not witnessed before. Our phase of life lies on the farther side of adulthood, mostly unseen and unknown to those of younger years. Let them see that we are mature and vital, compassionate and forgiving (mostly), loving and complex appreciators of this land beyond their view. Let them know that there is much more living to be discovered.

we have become a treasure chest

Renewing the treasure chest of age

Healthy aging can be viewed simply as a demonstration of love in action. We have become a treasure chest, shaped over our long lifetime of development and experience. Our older and matured brain provides us with a broadened field of vision and an accompanying capacity to understand more fully what we see. Our emotional experience has continued to mature as well, granting us a calm patience and a delicious quality of acceptance of life "as it is." As individuals, each of us has long been a "work in progress" that even now continues to cultivate these attributes associated with healthy aging. These attributes increasingly characterize who we have become at this point in our lives. These are the harvest of our aging.

We created these treasures of age through meaningful engagement with life, and renew and now sustain them by "spending" them in relationships with other people within our community. What we give to others is so frequently returned to us at this harvest time of life that we can hardly imagine being able to spend it all. Each time we put these rich treasures of age into service we also renew them within ourselves.

How will you renew the life treasures you carry, these rare and special qualities that reside within you now? Will it be through your role as a generous and non-judgmental grandparent, or a wise and patient mentor to younger people? Or, perhaps volunteering in important community activities that put your values into service for others? Sometimes the available avenues for sharing the bounty of our lives are not so clearly marked. Sometimes wisely allocating our talents requires creating new pathways for service that match our unique gifts.

The treasures of age that we offer are exactly what is most needed in today's society, and needed in abundance. Loving attention, gratitude, genuine good will toward others, patience and peacefulness are found primarily among our group of healthy agers. We maintain our healthy minds by using them fully and well. We preserve our emotional health by investing emotional energy in relationships with others. In this, we become the beneficiaries of the loving presence we offer others. Our active engagement in the life of our community, however we choose to express it, is a precious and necessary gift.

Life tastes different when we're older

Becoming "mature" is an ongoing process that ends finally in death. The continuously evolving interests and activities of older adults provide evidence for this position. Our experiences of what gives us pleasure or evokes fascination and excitement, or what contributes most to our sense of significance and meaning, continue to shift and change. We frequently discover that what was most interesting, exciting or important at 40 or 50 we often view quite differently at 70 or 80 (and what may be exciting at 70 or 80 may not even be on our radar at 40 or 50!).

Some of our changes in interest patterns relate to diminished physical energy that often accompanies aging. These are usually superficial changes, like continuing to enjoy skiing or golf, but now monitoring our energy more carefully on the slopes or the links and calling it a day earlier. Or we may still enjoy hiking, but withdraw from grueling treks through tough terrain. Aging teaches us to shepherd our physical energies more carefully.

Deeper changes come from more fundamental shifts in attitudes and perspectives that accompany on-going maturity. We may notice that we view social relationships differently. The pleasure we found in a swirl of social activities may be replaced by a desire for more quiet conversation with a smaller number of close friends. Or we may became more selective in our use of time as grandparents, choosing to limit time with grandchildren so as to not sacrifice favored "adult" pursuits with our own age mates. The older fellow with a moderate appetite for beer may become a "gourmet" who finds he now wants only one, but wants it flavorful and well made. And the recreational shopper may still enjoy that activity, but only with easy access to the right areas, spending her time perusing fewer, more carefully selected, items.

As we age our desire for quantity and variety is replaced by a desire for quality and depth. Fewer and richer experiences are more satisfying than a calendar filled with superficial contacts that fail to satisfy our itch for more meaningful engagement. Our desire for less glitter and more substance is evidence of emotional maturity. Tasting life through our refined sensibility is one of aging's rewards.

the trap of continuing to define ourselves by what we do

"Being" lies beyond busyness

Something often heard from older adults after they retire: "I'm busier now than when I was working." Yet unless we leave large open spaces in our post-retirement schedule we miss one of the greatest challenges and opportunities of aging—the opportunity to slow down enough to discover the life inside us.

Being busy can fill a space inside that might feel scary if we experience it only as emptiness. We are then tempted to stay busy just to avoid that feeling.

Adulthood is a training ground for busyness. Being busy has marked us as valuable people, doing necessary and important work. Our life worth is based on our capacity to be productive and contributing members of our community. If we are not "busy," than what value have we?

But the busyness of adult life now extends beyond working years, its clutches even reaching down to engulf the lives of children with scheduled after school activities, "play dates," music lessons, sports activities, all crowded into every available slot. Unstructured time becomes viewed as a menace; daydreaming and just "hanging out" viewed as temptations for straying into trouble.

Small wonder, then, that in our older adult years we are tempted to continue this same pattern of "productively" using our time just as we had always done throughout our adulthood. We easily fall into the trap of continuing to define ourselves by what we do, cheating ourselves out of any real experience of who we are beyond busyness, of who we are "inside."

Yet this change in definition, from myself as a "do-er" to myself as a "be-er" marks a major shift from adult life to a real experience of "elderhood." After an adulthood filled with busyness, we are now invited to a time beyond; a time to dream, to delve deeply into our inner life, with a reduced number of required outside activities. We have the space to "be" and the leisure to engage in unstructured "being" with others, including the opportunity to learn again how to "do nothing."

Aging focuses our engagement with being, an opportunity we have perhaps not fully exercised since we were children. Now, with our resources of life experience and time in these older years, we can explore again our inner landscape to discover what new adventures lie within.

Warmth and comfort within our memories

Our enhanced capacity to rekindle the fires of memories that nurture, comfort and support us is one of the advantages of being older. It is important that we encourage these visits we make into our past. We want not to dismiss people from our lives today who have been important parts of our history, have loved and cared for us, but are no longer living. We also want to rekindle nourishing experiences drawn from our relationship with nature. The traces of all those relationships remain inside our experience now, and can continue to nourish and strengthen us whenever we take the time to reflect upon them.

Experiences of pain and loneliness are at times a periodic visitor to any older person. We have by now loved and lost, perhaps several times over. There are people we miss and experiences we much enjoyed that we can no longer engage as before. We have every right, from time to time, to feel bad about that.

But we also know that this is only a part of the story of our lives. That we survived to this age testifies to our having been the receiver of the care of others. All of this nurture and care leaves markings in the library that is our memory. Gratefully, these continue as sources of support whenever we make a visit.

The experiences of nurture now housed in memory are not imagined fantasies—they actually occurred—and because they did, our lives were strengthened and supported. The parent who sacrificed for our well being, the teacher who saw something in us and inspired us, the friend who stood by us when we needed support, the woodland hikes we loved; all these are nourishing memories that remain alive inside us.

Our experience of these riches within our memories contributes to the legacy that we pass along to many others in our lives. We have been and continue to be the positive figures within the memories of those we have cared for and are caring for now. We rank among the sources of nurture and support for members of our families and circle of friends, available to them on those lonely occasions that will inevitably arise in their lives. We, too, are housed in the libraries of their warm and nurturing memories.

the experiences of nurture now housed in our memories

With age: Greater sensitivity and the wisdom to use it well

A word that frequently crops up to describe older people is "vulnerable," usually with a negative connotation. Unwisely giving money to shaky causes and predatory relatives, or falling victim to scams. Perhaps falling into patterns of excessive worry, often about the well being of someone we care about but are unable to help in any significant way.

Yet an increasing experience of emotional vulnerability is actually a sign of the maturity that accompanies aging. We become more emotionally expressive, are able to show more sensitivity and care for others, and can feel more deeply connected with those in relationships particularly important to us.

But our greater sensitivity carries some greater risks. We become less insulated from painful experiences, both in our own lives and in the lives of the people close to us. We feel more the "pain of the world" presented in the on-going news cycles that bombard us. And, as noted above, we are more susceptible to the pulls of mean spirited people who talk of noble causes but really only want our money, or to the pain we hear in the lives of friends and family. Because we are more emotionally available than ever before, we can, if not careful, become battered and abused.

Some older people protectively shut themselves down to avoid just such pain. When someone suffers and we can't do much about it, it's tempting to close ourselves off. We may refuse the work of erecting needed emotional boundaries and simply throw the switch and disconnect altogether. It's hard to say "no" when someone we care about wants our time, attention, or money even when they pay little heed to our fatigue, exhaustion, or quite limited resources.

Fortunately our enhanced maturity serves us well here. Through our aging, wisdom has increasingly become the natural partner to our expanded sensitivity. Yes, we are more able to feel more deeply and to express care and concern for others. Yet we are also increasingly capable of making wise choices. Our experience, carefully considered, has taught us discernment. With age, impulsive actions that might hurt us give way to careful and reasoned reflection. This forms the mental basis for the important self care needed to guide the actions of our more sensitive and compassionate heart.

Finding the money

It's a common story, one most of us who have gone through the painful process of settling a parent's or relative's estate know from personal experience. A parent or close relative moves toward the end of life. We're caught in our own grief while trying to pay attention to health care declarations and seeing that other personal legal documents are up to date. Mostly we just want to spend the best "quality" time we can with this person before they die.

Then, following the death, the game of financial treasure hunting commences. There are some stocks, but where? Bank accounts can be easier to locate, but do we really know we have everything even there? Were there other resources, like CDs (certificates of deposit), somewhere? As we delve earnestly into the hunt, other questions arise that we should have asked when we could, or would have asked if we'd been invited to. They are questions about facts, yet laden with difficult emotion.

Maybe we were embarrassed to ever raise direct questions about financial matters, deeming them inappropriate or impolite (especially when the person is seriously ill or dying!). Or, sudden death may have taken away any such opportunity. Nonetheless, we simply didn't find out beforehand, and now we're in frantic search mode.

That's when we realize we should have stiffened our backbone and brought these questions up much earlier, even when these important elders were still in relatively good health. We realize, too, how much we would have welcomed that older person's opening this conversation with us, making financial affairs something easier and more comfortable to discuss. We vow not to repeat this error with our own children, or those to whom we feel some responsibility for sharing the intimate details of our own financial lives.

But have we actually done this, or have we found it easier to postpone the awkward and delicate subject of nailing down financial resources? Are we waiting for the "right time" (just when is that!)? How much anguish and hassle do we want to inflict on those whom we love and count on to expedite our remaining resources after our death? If we remember what the struggle to piece the financial puzzle together was like for us, we might recognize that this process cannot begin too soon.

we were embarrassed to raise direct questions about financial matters

Glad to be alive!

The work of the neurologist and writer Oliver Sacks has been followed by many older people, not simply because of our collective interest in how our minds function, but also because his writing has been so direct and accessible. Recently Dr. Sacks published an article about his own impending entrance into his eighth decade. He called it, "The Joy of Old Age.(No Kidding)." His description of his experience of growing older give us all a model of what we mean when talking about "healthy aging."

It is important to note that Dr. Sacks, at approaching 80, does not claim perfect health. He describes instead a "scattering of medical and surgical problems, none disabling... I feel glad to be alive." Those of us who have followed his career know that this "scattering" to which he refers includes a stroke, the loss of vision in one eye, and significant hearing loss. Yet he remains grateful for the life he has been given, the work he has chosen, and the friendships he has cultivated along the way.

Dr. Sacks relates his optimism about growing older to the attitude demonstrated by his own father, who claimed that:

> "The 80s had been one of the most enjoyable decades of his life. He felt, as I begin to feel, not a shrinking but an enlargement of mental life and perspective... One is more conscious of transience and, perhaps, of beauty. At 80, one can take a long view and have a vivid, lived sense of history not possible at an earlier age."

Such generous optimism in the face of physical limitation is not a "put on" attitude but actually arises from the richness of his own experience of life. In closing Dr. Sacks says,

> "I do not think of old age as an ever grimmer time that one must somehow endure and make the best of, but as a time of leisure and freedom, freed from the fractitious urgency of earlier days, free to explore whatever I wish, and to bind the thoughts and feelings of a lifetime together."

Here are more than just the reflections of one creative and compassionate man, "looking forward to being 80." Oliver Sachs illustrates an attitude available to us all: open hearted generosity, a broadened perspective, and a continuing zest for living.

to bind the thoughts and feelings of a lifetime together

Living in peace

Someone's quiet radiance beckons and quickly invites our attention: we come into the presence of an older person exuding a powerful sense of being at peace and entirely at home in their own skin. When with them, we, too, experience a sense of comfort in our own being. We feel better, easier and lighter with ourselves, just soaking up their company.

When we pay attention and notice how they "operate," we find ourselves drawn mostly to what it is that they don't do, less so what they do. We notice that they appear remarkably non-judgmental of others. They seem not particularly prone to convincing anyone else to be anything other than they already are. They also seem totally uninterested in turning anyone else into any near version of themselves.

We see that they are at peace within themselves. Looking in from the outside, we are compelled to wonder how they achieved this state? If being at peace defines successful living, what's the secret of their success?

Fortunately for us, the qualities that mark a movement toward peacefulness within life are greatly enhanced by the process of aging. With greater emotional maturity, we bear witness to and accept the life choices and life events that have brought us to the point in our life's journey. In healthy aging, uncritical self-acceptance is the luscious "fruit" from our harvest of age. The critical voice of mid-life that reminded us to "be more" and "be better" now gives way to a gentle self-acceptance. We greet the wrinkled face reflected back to us in the mirror now not with scorn but with warmth and humor, even to affirm "I know you—this is who I am" with no changes necessary nor desired. With self-acceptance, all of the competitive characteristics of mid-life fall away and the quest for possessions and performing for another's approval increasingly dissolve.

As these disappear from our landscape, so does any strong pull to be elsewhere rather than "here," or to find any better people than those beside now us. "More," "better," and "different" carry little allure now. We rest in our own good company, and it is quite enough. This is the personification of successful aging—being fully at home in our own skin.

we greet the face in the mirror— "I know you - this is who I am"

Afterward

Aging into mystery

Every stage of life carries with it some defining beginning and end. From birth to death, we have external markers signaling when we become an adolescent, a young adult, a middle ager, an older adult. Increasingly, we also have access to the view from the inside of each of these phases. We know more now than formerly about how adults see the world and their place in it. We are only beginning to similarly know the inner experience of those of us living closer to the end of the continuum of life.

Here lies the journey into mystery. Those whose experience has progressed late into aging have sailed off the shores of the known world toward a landscape that lies beyond our capacity to reckon with any degree of certainty. Fortunately, our capacity to tolerate unknownness has increased just as it has become most necessary. We are prepared for this journey with values tested through time and experience and with skills and capacities honed through the many choices we have made along the way. The presence of mystery, always slyly resting at the edges of our awareness at each stage of life, now asserts itself into the very center of our experience. Attending to its call, we know there is more yet to discover.

Acknowledgments

Any effort of this scope has "hidden helpers." Principle among them is Dianne Aisenbrey, the highly organized and efficient task master and editorial assistant whose steady hand kept us moving forward with this project. Given a couple of rather distractible characters like ourselves, Dianne's was a pivotal role.

Robin's husband/photo assistant, Keith, also provided invaluable encouragement and support throughout this project, as did her parents and all those who allowed her to photograph them for this book.

Thanks, too, to the numerous older adults who have woven through our lives over the last decade, who have touched our lives in ways that have enlightened and inspired us. We have appreciated our connection with the Red Wing Area Seniors programs, special projects developed with Goodhue County Health & Human Services, the Red Wing Housing and Redevelopment Agency and Pine Island Area Home Services, among others. The depth of shared experiences of aging formed the basis for these essays and the inspiration for the photography that accompanies them here.